TEEN LIFE™

FREQUENTLY ASKED QUESTIONS ABOUT

Emergency Lifesaving Techniques

Greg Roza

ROSEN
PUBLISHING®

New York

Published in 2010 by The Rosen Publishing Group, Inc.
29 East 21st Street, New York, NY 10010

Copyright © 2010 by The Rosen Publishing Group, Inc.

First Edition

Library of Congress Cataloging-in-Publication Data

Roza, Greg.
Frequently asked questions about emergency lifesaving techniques / Greg Roza.
    p. cm.—(FAQ: teen life)
Includes bibliographical references and index.
ISBN-13: 978-1-4358-5327-0 (library binding)
1. First aid in illness and injury—Juvenile literature.
2. Lifesaving—Juvenile literature. I. Title.
RC86.5.R69 2010
616.02'52—dc22

                                                    2008055401

Manufactured in the United States of America

Contents

WHAT ARE THE BASIC TECHNIQUES OF EMERGENCY LIFESAVING?

Would you know what to do if your friend broke a bone while skateboarding? What would you do if your brother burned himself while your parents were out of the house? Do you know what shock is and how to treat a person who experiences it after an accident? Do you know the proper way to treat hypothermia? No one wants to think about situations like these, but chances are we will all find ourselves in one eventually.

The way we respond to accidents could mean the difference between a quick recovery and a life-threatening injury. A lot can happen in the time that it takes an EMT (emergency medical technician), nurse, or doctor to respond to an emergency. Being prepared to administer first aid can help reduce the damage that results from an accident.

Calling 911

The most important step when administering lifesaving first aid is getting professional help as soon as possible. One person should call 911 as first aid is being performed by others on the scene. If you are in a group of people, designate one specific person by pointing at or calling him or her by name and ask him or her to call 911 immediately. If you are alone, it's almost always best to call 911 before quickly beginning to administer first aid.

When calling for help, be prepared to relate as much information as possible. Remain calm and speak clearly. If possible, stay on the phone until help arrives. You'll want to give the following information when calling 911:

- What happened
- Victim's injuries or symptoms
- Victim's present state (breathing, consciousness, etc.)
- When the injury occurred
- Victim's location
- Victim's medications
- In the case of poisoning, what substance was taken, the amount, and how long ago
- Phone numbers where you can be reached

Even though this book is meant to make you more able to help out in an emergency, it can't prepare you for everything. Everyone should take a certified first-aid training course. Your

Do you enjoy outdoor activities such as biking? No matter how good you are, accidents can happen. Would you know how to respond if this happened to you?

local Red Cross offers several different kinds of emergency training, including basic first aid, CPR (cardiopulmonary resuscitation), babysitter's training, sports safety training, and pet first aid.

The information in this book is most useful when it's paired with proper first-aid training. In fact, there are some emergency practices discussed in this book that you simply shouldn't attempt if you don't have proper training. Turn to the section at the end of this book titled "For More Information" to find Red Cross–sponsored first-aid training in your community.

Emergency medical technicians respond to the scene of a bicycle accident. While waiting for the ambulance, you can help out by assessing the victim's injuries, applying basic first aid, and making the person as comfortable as possible.

Basic First-Aid Supplies

You can never anticipate ahead of time what type of accident you'll get involved in, so it's best to have a variety of first-aid supplies on hand. The first thing you should do is put together a first-aid kit containing the most basic supplies: adhesive bandages, sterile gauze, medical tape, sterile gloves, antibiotic cream, hand sanitizer and/or soap, disinfectant wipes, burn ointment, ice pack, and scissors. You may also want to keep the following items handy in case of an emergency:

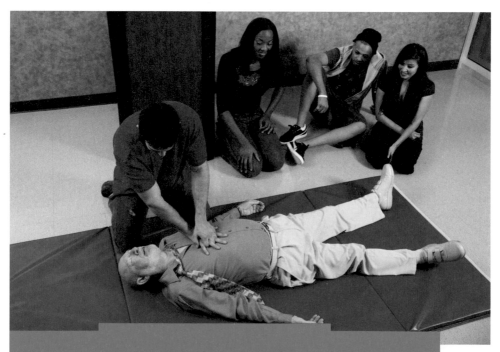

These teens are taking a course in first aid. In this picture, they are learning how to administer CPR to an unconscious adult.

- Pain relievers, like ibuprofen or acetaminophen (children should NEVER take aspirin)
- A supply of any prescription medication that you normally take
- Hydrocortisone cream (to treat itching)
- Diphenhydramine (Benadryl) in case of hives or another allergic reaction
- Eyewash
- Cotton swabs
- Tweezers
- Flashlight
- Drinking water
- Thermometer
- Blanket
- Towels
- Cell phone and emergency numbers

Being prepared with a well-stocked first-aid kit kept in your car or backpack allows you to begin treating victims of an accident or illness quickly, providing essential aid in those crucial minutes when you wait for an ambulance to arrive. In more serious accidents, you might even be helping a victim stay alive long enough for the EMTs to arrive and begin their lifesaving work.

Check ABC

Preparing for emergencies is just the first step. Should an emergency occur, you need to act quickly and decisively. The term

"ABC" is one of the most useful ways of remembering how to respond to an emergency or accident. The letters stand for Airway, Breathing, and Circulation. These are sometimes called the vital signs. Some prefer the abbreviation "Dr. ABC." The "D" and "R" stand for Danger Response. This means you should always examine the surroundings for dangerous situations before turning your attention to the victim. For example, you don't want to rush over to a victim of electrical shock until you are sure that there are no open or "live" electrical wires in the area.

One other word of warning: the only time you should refrain from moving a victim away from a dangerous area is when he or she may have a neck or spinal injury. Moving the person may increase the damage and may even cause permanent paralysis. As in all emergency situations, get the help of a professional as soon as possible. Cover the victim with a blanket or jackets to prevent shock, and stay with him or her until help arrives.

Airway

The airway is the passage that runs between the nose, mouth, and lungs. When this passage is blocked, breathing will be difficult or even impossible. When first helping someone who is injured, make sure that his or her airway is clear. If the person is conscious, ask if he or she can breathe. (See chapter 2 for further information on how to treat choking.) If the person is unconscious (and he or she does not have a neck or spinal injury), lay the person flat, tip the chin up with one hand, and use your other hand to tilt the head back. Sweep your finger through the back of his or her mouth to check for an obstruction (something blocking or clogging the airway).

Breathing and Circulation

To check someone's breathing, lean close to his or her mouth to listen for the sound of breath being drawn in and out. To check for the victim's heartbeat, place the index and middle fingers of your hand on his or her wrist or throat and try to find the pulse. If you feel it, that means the heart is still beating. If the person's skin is pale or splotchy, he or she may have a problem with circulation. The person's pulse should be slow but steady. If the person is not breathing or has no pulse, someone must perform rescue breathing and CPR until the patient is breathing again. (See chapter 2 for more information about rescue breathing and CPR.)

The Three Bs

Some health-care professionals also suggest following the rule of three Bs: Breathing, Bleeding, Bones. First check for breathing, using the same methods discussed above. Once you are sure the victim is breathing, check the pulse and make sure that the person is not bleeding. If the person is bleeding, apply direct, steady pressure to all wounds to stop it. Once you have addressed breathing and bleeding, carefully examine the victim to make sure that he or she has no broken bones.

Sometimes a bandage is all the first aid you need to administer. Still, always make sure the wound is clean and clear of debris before applying a bandage.

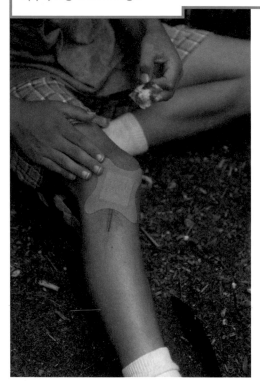

The Recovery Position

If the person you are treating is unconscious or semiconscious, you should place him or her in the "recovery position" while awaiting medical help. This position will keep the person's airway open and allow any blood or other fluids to drain out of his or her mouth and nose.

While the person is lying on his or her back, stretch the arm closest to you away from his or her body perpendicularly, and place the back of the farther hand under the person's near cheek. Next, grab the person's far knee and gently roll the person toward you onto his or her side so that the face is resting on the hand. Make sure the person's head is tilted up and the airway is clear. Cover the person with a coat or blanket unless he or she is suffering an overheating or heat-related illness.

Treating Shock

You may have heard someone say that an injured person is "going into shock." This means that the stress of the situation has caused the person to experience certain physical and emotional symptoms, such as disorientation, confusion, agitation, panic, sweating, flushed skin, and amnesia. Symptoms can last for hours or even days. The real scientific term for this condition is called acute stress reaction.

Physicians also use the term "shock" (short for circulatory shock) to refer to a more dangerous condition where the blood does not circulate properly, and the organs thus do not receive enough oxygen, which is carried by the red blood cells. This condition can result in organ damage and death if not treated immediately. Shock can result from numerous injuries and illnesses, including persistent bleeding, heart disorders, allergic reactions, burns, heatstroke, and poisoning.

The symptoms of circulatory shock can include cold and clammy skin, thirst, restlessness, nervousness, nausea, confusion, fast and weak heartbeat, rapid breathing, and unconsciousness. If you suspect that someone is experiencing circulatory shock, call 911 immediately. While waiting for the ambulance, have the person lie flat with his or her feet higher than the head to improve blood flow to the brain. Frequently check to make sure that the person is breathing, especially if he or she is unconscious. Loosen tight clothing. Do not give the person anything to drink, even if he or she asks for water.

WHAT ARE AIRWAY MANAGEMENT AND CPR?

The two most important concerns when administering first aid to someone are the person's breathing and blood flow. A problem with either function can result in a deficiency of oxygen in the blood, called hypoxemia. If this situation is not remedied as soon as possible it will result in organ failure and death. Regardless of the nature of the injury, you should constantly monitor the victim's breathing and heart rate. If you fail to do so, you may miss a more serious condition.

Again it must be mentioned that these methods are best applied by trained professionals, or at least by someone with proper first-aid training. The information here is merely a start. Check with your local Red Cross for classes to receive proper training in CPR, rescue breathing, AED (automated external defibrillator), and other first-aid techniques. In the end, it's usually better to

The woman in this picture is administering mouth-to-mouth resuscitation—also called rescue breathing—to an unconscious boy. Together, rescue breathing and CPR have been used to save countless lives.

avoid using these techniques if you aren't sure how to do them properly, rather than doing them and causing more harm to the victim.

Rescue Breathing

Rescue breathing, commonly called mouth-to-mouth resuscitation, is used to treat someone who has stopped breathing. This can occur as a result of an accident, electrocution, poisoning, allergic reaction, near drowning, and other incidents. When someone has stopped breathing, you can use rescue breathing to breathe for him or her.

Begin by laying the person on his or her back on a stable surface. Tilt the head back by placing one hand under the neck and lifting the chin with the other hand. Once the mouth is open, look inside. If you can see any solid obstruction, sweep your fingers through the mouth to remove it. Next, quickly check for normal breathing. Watch the victim's chest, listen for breathing, and feel for breath coming from the nose or mouth with your hand. Gasping and a lack of breathing are signs that rescue breathing may be necessary.

Use one hand to keep the person's chin tipped up and the other to hold the victim's forehead still. Pinch the person's nostrils closed, with the heel of your hand resting on his or her forehead. Inhale deeply and blow a full breath into the person's mouth. You can also blow air through the nose if the person has a mouth injury. Turn your head to the side as you draw another breath and listen for air coming out of the person's mouth. If the person's chest doesn't move up and down or you can't hear him or her exhale, check the airway again to make sure it's clear.

Give one breath every five seconds for adults and one breath every three seconds for children. Great care must be taken when administering rescue breathing to infants. Use much smaller breaths. Continue this process until the person is breathing on his or her own or until help arrives. Rescue breathing is often combined with chest compressions (see CPR section below).

CPR

Cardiopulmonary resuscitation (CPR) is a lifesaving technique that is applied when someone's heart has stopped beating. CPR has two main steps: rescue breathing and chest compressions. This procedure keeps oxygenated blood flowing to the brain until the person's heart begins beating again or until a medical professional can administer more effective treatment. The brain will suffer irreparable damage in just a few minutes without oxygen. Death occurs between eight and ten minutes without oxygen. There are different methods of CPR for adults and children.

Before performing CPR, check the condition of the person. If the person seems unconscious, tap his or her shoulder and ask loudly, "Are you OK?" If the person doesn't respond, have someone call 911 immediately while you begin CPR. If you are alone, call 911 first and then perform CPR.

First, make sure that the person's airway is clear. Then, check to see if the person is breathing. If the person isn't breathing, begin rescue breathing. The next step is to perform chest compressions to restore blood circulation. Place the heel of one hand on the person's chest, and place the other over it. Push down on the person's chest, compressing about one-third of chest depth. Do thirty quick compressions, followed by two quick, big breaths into the person's mouth (while pinching the nose). It is very important that you received proper CPR training to avoid further injuring or otherwise harming the victim.

What to Do When Someone Is Choking

Choking occurs when an object becomes lodged in the trachea, thereby preventing air from entering or leaving the lungs. People sometimes choke on food. Children may choke on small toys or balloons that they accidentally inhale. Infants and toddlers can easily choke on small, round foods like peanuts, grapes, and candy.

Signs that someone is choking include gasping, coughing, difficulty speaking or inability to speak, blue lips and face, and grasping of the throat. If you suspect that someone is choking, the first thing you should do is ask, "Are you OK?" or "Are you choking?" If the person nods or can't respond, it's time to act. Since a quick reaction is the most important response for someone who is choking, administering first aid is more important than calling 911. Choking incidents can be taken care of quickly, and medical help may not be necessary or may arrive too late. Still, someone should be prepared to call 911 if first aid doesn't help the choking victim quickly.

Dr. Henry Heimlich demonstrates the Heimlich maneuver to an audience of students in California. Dr. Heimlich began advocating abdominal thrusts as a treatment for choking in the mid-1970s.

If the victim is coughing, encourage him or her to continue doing so. Strong coughing is often enough to expel the object that is lodged in the person's throat. If the person can't cough, abdominal thrusts are necessary to help dislodge the obstruction. Abdominal thrusts are also called the Heimlich maneuver. Stand behind the person and wrap your arms around his or her stomach. Make a fist with one hand and place it above the person's navel and below the ribcage, with your fingers against the abdomen. Place your other hand over your fist. Make sure that the person is bent slightly forward to be able to expel the object. Quickly press in and up as if you were trying to lift the person off the ground. This action compresses the lungs and applies pressure to the obstruction in the trachea, hopefully forcing the obstruction out. The thrusts must be quick and forceful. Repeat until the blockage is forced out.

Other Methods of Treating Choking Victims

There are times when the regular Heimlich maneuver is not appropriate and another method must be employed. If the person becomes unconscious, lay him or her on the floor face up. Straddle the person's waist, facing him or her. Place the heel of one hand above the victim's navel and place your other hand over it. Using your body weight, push down and up until the blockage is expelled.

For infants, place them on the ground at your knees or hold them on your lap, facing away from you. Place the middle and index fingers of both hands above the navel and below the ribcage. Quickly, but very gently, press in and up. Do not press on the ribcage.

If you are choking and there is no one nearby to help you, make a fist with one hand and place it against your abdomen above your navel, thumb inside. Place your other hand over it and quickly push in and up. Or lean your abdomen against the back of a chair or railing and quickly push yourself against it.

HOW DO I TREAT WOUNDS, BLEEDING, AND BROKEN BONES?

Everyone is familiar with the occasional cut or scrape that occurs during ordinary daily activities. These minor injuries don't always require a trip to the hospital. But more serious accidents like punctures, fractures, broken bones, and bleeding may.

Puncture Wounds

Sharp objects like nails and tacks cause puncture wounds. Puncture wounds should be disinfected and bandaged just like regular cuts and scrapes. However, puncture wounds can cause more damage depending on how deep they go. They also carry a greater risk of contracting tetanus. This is because it's hard or impossible to properly clean a deep puncture

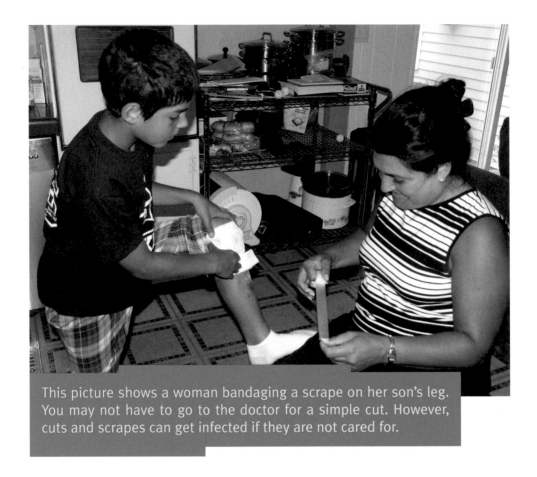

This picture shows a woman bandaging a scrape on her son's leg. You may not have to go to the doctor for a simple cut. However, cuts and scrapes can get infected if they are not cared for.

wound. See a doctor instead of trying to clean a dirty puncture wound yourself.

Animal Bites

Animal bites are also considered puncture wounds. While waiting for medical attention, thoroughly cleanse the wound with soap and a lot of water. You should always see a doctor after being bitten by a stray or neglected dog or a wild animal because there is a risk of contracting rabies. Animal species that carry rabies differ depending on the area, but be especially careful around raccoons, bats, skunks, foxes, and coyotes. Always contact your local animal control department so it can catch the animal before anyone else gets bitten. If you think you or someone you know may have contracted rabies, seek immediate medical attention. If a doctor thinks that you have been infected, he or she will give you a series of immunization shots. Do not delay seeking treatment. Once symptoms appear—which may take a few months—rabies is always fatal.

Severe Bleeding

Serious accidents or trauma can cause severe bleeding. Sometimes even smaller cuts won't stop bleeding. It's important for you to keep your cool when administering first aid to someone who is experiencing severe bleeding. The person is likely to be distraught and in great pain. If you panic, he or she probably will, too, which can make the bleeding worse.

Call 911 and have the injured person lie down with his or her head lower than the rest of the body. This will keep blood flowing to the brain and will reduce the chance of fainting and shock. Elevate the injured area if you can to help reduce bleeding.

If possible, wash your hands and put on a pair of latex gloves. Quickly inspect the wound and remove any foreign bodies. But it's vital to apply pressure to the wound as soon as possible. Use a sterile cloth or gauze if you can. Keep the pressure constant for at least twenty minutes. Don't take your hands away to check the wound. You may need to bind the wound with a long bandage or

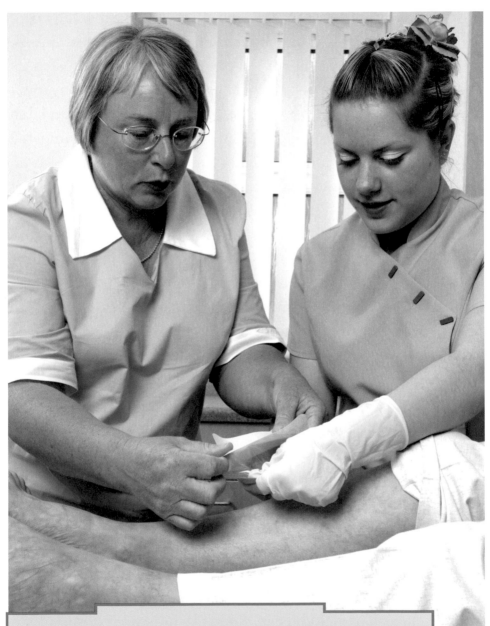

A nurse and a health-care assistant work together to change the bandages on a patient's leg. Changing bandages regularly is important to help a wound heal properly and to help avoid infection.

a cloth. If blood soaks through the material that you're using, don't remove it. Instead, apply a new layer of material over it and keep holding pressure.

Sometimes it's necessary to squeeze a main artery against the bone to help stop the bleeding. This reduces the amount of blood that is pumped to the wounded area. For an arm injury, the main arteries are on the inside of the arm, just above the elbow and just below the armpit. For leg injuries, the main arteries are located on the back of the knee and in the groin.

If the wound is in the area of the abdomen, watch for displaced organs. Don't move organs that have slipped outside the body or try to push them back in. Cover them with a towel or sterile gauze, and try to keep the person still.

Internal Bleeding

Some injuries may result in internal bleeding. Signs of internal bleeding include bleeding from the ears, nose, or mouth; vomiting blood; bruises on the neck, chest, or abdomen; and shock. There isn't much you can do in these cases, but it's very important to call 911 immediately and have the person lie still while waiting for medical help to arrive.

Bone Injuries

The way to treat a broken bone depends on the type of break. It's important to treat a broken bone properly, with the appropriate method, to avoid further damage. In general, however, it's best not to treat broken bones unless you absolutely have to. In fact, you shouldn't move someone who has a broken bone unless his or her life is in danger. The following advice will help you treat various bone injuries while waiting for a medical professional to arrive.

Fractures

Fractures are usually not very dangerous, though they can be extremely painful. Yet, fractures can lead to dangerous infections or serious bleeding if they are left untreated or are not treated properly.

A fracture may look swollen and bruised, or the bone may break through the skin. Unless you have been trained to prepare a splint, never try to realign a broken bone. Wait for a medical professional. Gently support the injured area with padding, if possible. Wrap ice in a towel and gently apply it to the area to reduce swelling. You may need to treat the victim for shock. In the case of an open fracture, gently apply pressure to stop bleeding. Build up soft, sterile bandages around the wound and wrap it with more bandages. Just remember that moving a broken bone can cause greater damage, so do it only when the victim's life is in danger.

A dislocation is a displacement of the bones that meet at a joint. Dislocations often happen to the shoulders, fingers, and jaw. But they may happen to bones in other areas as well. Follow the same advice for broken bones. Moving or trying to reset a dislocation can result in worse damage. This is especially true in the case of dislocated bones of the spine. In the

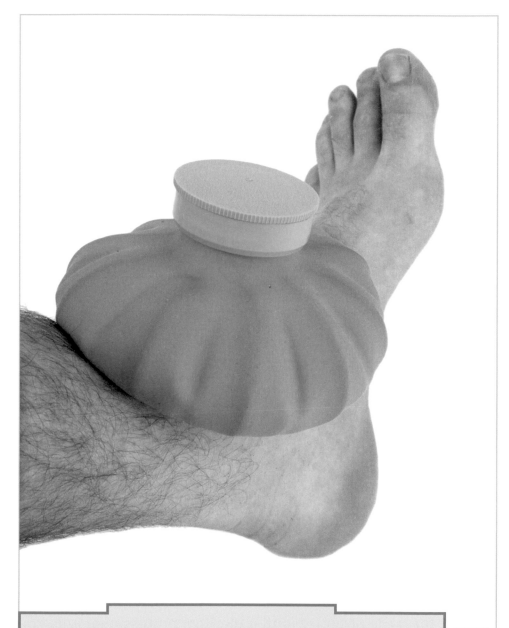

Ice can help reduce swelling when someone has a broken bone. However, be as careful as you can when applying ice so as not to cause the victim unnecessary pain.

event of bone dislocation, try to make the victim as comfortable as possible while waiting for medical help. Then let the professionals take over and perform the bone resetting or administer other treatment.

Types of Fractures	
Fracture	**Description**
Simple	A single break in the bone
Comminuted	Multiple fractures or breaks in the bone
Open	A completely broken bone breaks through the skin, creating a wound that bleeds
Closed	A completely broken bone does not break the skin but can cause swelling and bruising
Greenstick	A fracture that does not go all the way through the bone; common in children because their bones are more pliable than adult bones

Head, Neck, and Back Injuries

Head, neck, and back injuries must be treated with great care to avoid causing worse problems. In fact, if you ever find an injured person who is unconscious, it's best to assume that he or she has this type of injury until a medical professional tells you otherwise.

Symptoms of a head injury include cuts or bruises on the head; dizziness; confusion; difficulty speaking; fluids running from the ears, nose, or mouth; headache; vomiting; pupils of uneven size; and unconsciousness. Head injuries are often accompanied by neck injuries, so it's important to keep the person as still as possible. Call 911, and keep the victim calm and lying down. Monitor vital signs until help arrives. Control blood flow only if it's serious, but be very gentle and do not move the victim.

The only time that you should move someone with a neck or back injury is when he or she is in imminent danger, as from a fire or a collapsing building. Doing so without a trained medical professional's help can result in greater damage, permanent paralysis, and even death. Symptoms of neck injuries include headache, stiffness, inability to move a part of the body, and tingling in the hands and feet. Symptoms of a back injury include the inability to move body parts or move at all, and tingling in the neck, back, arms, and/or legs.

If you can, call 911 immediately and wait for the EMTs to arrive. You can place tightly folded blankets or towels next to the person's head, neck, and sides to keep him or her from moving. Stay calm and keep the person warm. If you absolutely have to perform CPR or move the person, do what you can to keep his or her body perfectly straight. Bending or twisting the victim's body can cause lasting damage.

four

HOW DO I TREAT POISONING?

There are many different kinds of poisons in our world, and many different types of symptoms and reactions. This makes poisoning difficult for the average person to treat. In cases of poisoning, always call 911 or poison control. The American Association of Poison Control Centers (AAPCC) is a private organization representing the sixty-one poison control centers (PCCs) in the United States. This organization manages a twenty-four-hour poison hotline. The number is (800) 222-1222.

Poisoning is caused by ingesting, inhaling, injecting, or absorbing a substance that is harmful to the body. Most cases of poisoning are accidents. According to a report generated from a data center maintained by the AAPCC, more than 2.4 million people called the poison hotline to report cases of human exposure to poisons in 2006. The most common substances involved in these cases were analgesics (pain relievers). About 1,200 of all reported poisoning cases resulted in death (1 out of every 2,000 reported poison victims). A quick response to poisoning is very important and can help to greatly reduce injuries and death.

Ingestion

Ingested poisons can include foods, alcohol, medications, cosmetics, household chemicals, and even plants. Look for the following symptoms: residue or redness around the mouth, difficulty breathing and talking, vomiting, gagging, coughing, stomach pain, and unusual breath.

If someone you know has swallowed poison, call 911 or poison control immediately, even if symptoms don't initially appear. The operator will want to know what poison was swallowed, how much, and how long ago. The operator may ask you to have the person drink milk or water to dilute the poison. Which liquid the person is told to drink depends on the poison, so don't administer anything without being told to. If the person vomits, use a cloth to clean the poison out of the mouth. It may sound gross, but you should also collect the vomited material to bring with you to the emergency room for inspection. Remove any clothing that may have poison on it.

Induced (forced and intentional) vomiting was once recommended as a treatment for most poison ingestion. However, it's no longer considered an effective means of treating all forms of poisoning. Some poisons burn the throat

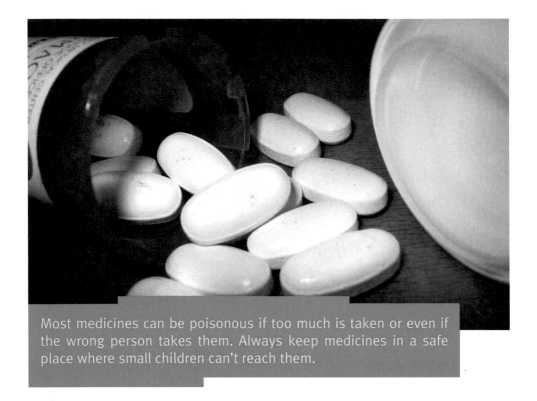

Most medicines can be poisonous if too much is taken or even if the wrong person takes them. Always keep medicines in a safe place where small children can't reach them.

as they are swallowed. They can burn the throat again when vomiting is induced. Some vomited poisons can enter the lungs and damage them. A poison control operator may tell you to induce vomiting. Do this only when instructed to by a medical professional.

Inhalation

Inhaled poisons include carbon monoxide (a major component of car exhaust), carbon dioxide, smoke, and chemical vapors. Symptoms of inhalation poisoning depend on the poison, but they may include the following: headache, confusion, nausea, vomiting, difficulty breathing, coughing, choking, and unconsciousness.

Poison inhalation is particularly serious when the tissues of the lungs become damaged. Quickly move the victim away from the source of the poisoning as soon as you can, and be very careful not to breathe in the poison yourself. Open all windows and doors if you are stuck inside. Call 911 or poison control, and try to identify the poison so that you can tell the operator. Bring the person to a well-ventilated area and check his or her breathing and heart rate. Be prepared to administer CPR until help arrives.

Absorption

Substances that can be absorbed into the skin include drugs and wet and dry industrial chemicals. Some plants, such as poison oak and poison ivy, often enter the body through the skin, but they usually do not require immediate medical attention. Symptoms of poison absorption may include redness, rash, swelling, chemical burns, and blisters.

If someone you know gets a poisonous substance on himself or herself, be careful not to get it on yourself also when trying to help. Call 911. Flush the area with lots of water for about fifteen minutes. Remove any contaminated clothing and throw it away. Wash the area with soap and water. (See chapter 5 for treating chemical burns.)

The eyes absorb poisons very quickly, which can lead to eye damage in just minutes. Rinse the victim's eyes with lukewarm water for at least fifteen minutes. Allow the person to blink his or her eyes frequently, and do not force the eyelids open. If pain, blurriness, or blindness ensues, see a doctor immediately.

Injection

Poisons can be injected into the body via a hypodermic needle. These can include ordinarily therapeutic medicines like insulin for diabetics or illegal drugs like heroin. Putting too many of these drugs into your body can result in an overdose. Symptoms of an overdose depend on the drug, but they may include weakness, dizziness, hallucinations, anxiety, unconsciousness, and coma. Call 911 immediately in the case of poisoning by injection, and monitor the person's vital signs until help arrives.

Bee stings and venomous snakebites are forms of poisonous injections. Often, insect bites and snakebites are painful but nothing to worry about. Some spider bites and snakebites, however, can be very poisonous. And for those who are allergic to them, bee stings can be life threatening. Symptoms of such stings and bites may include nausea, sweating, muscle cramps, weakness, swelling, and difficulty breathing. You can call 911 or poison control if you or a friend is stung or bitten and a strong reaction follows.

Remain calm while awaiting help, and keep the bite lower than the heart to decrease the flow of venom. If it's safe, save the bug or snake so that a medical professional can inspect it. Some stings and bites can cause an allergic reaction called anaphylactic shock (covered later in this chapter). This can be treated with a shot of adrenaline (epinephrine), steroids, and/or an oral antihistamine if you are prepared for such an emergency.

Smoke inhalation during a fire is a common form of poisoning. This woman, who was saved from a burning building, is being treated for smoke inhalation.

Alcohol Poisoning

When someone drinks too much alcohol in a short period of time, that person can poison himself or herself. This usually happens as a result of binge drinking. Since alcohol poisoning affects the central nervous system, it can lead to unconsciousness, coma, and death. It can also inhibit the gag reflex, causing an inebriated person to choke on his or her own vomit.

If you think someone you know has alcohol poisoning, call 911 or poison control immediately and monitor the person until help arrives. You may need to administer CPR.

Allergic Reactions

An allergic reaction is the body's way of responding to an invading threat. That threat may come from food, medications, plants, dust, mold, chemicals, animal bites and stings, and other sources. Although allergens are not really poisons, they can have similar effects on some people. If you or someone close to you has a known allergy, ask your doctor how to prepare for and combat an allergic reaction.

The biggest concern with allergic reactions is anaphylactic shock—a full-body, potentially deadly allergic reaction. The most common causes are foods, drugs, and insect stings. Symptoms often develop within seconds. They include difficulty breathing, coughing, stomach cramps, anxiety, confusion, dizziness, fainting, hives, nausea, vomiting, and heart palpitations. In the worst cases, respiratory failure and cardiac arrest can occur.

Call 911 immediately if you think someone is experiencing anaphylactic shock. Monitor his or her vital signs and be prepared to administer CPR. People with a known serious allergic reaction may already have an allergy kit with them. Most contain an injectable shot of adrenaline (epinephrine; commonly called an EpiPen) to be administered into the thigh muscle. This helps counteract the reaction and can be life-saving. If you or someone you know has a serious allergic reaction, you should understand how to use an allergy kit.

Ten Great Questions to Ask an Emergency Medical Technician (EMT)

1 What is the proper way to administer CPR?

2 What is the proper way to administer rescue breathing?

3 What phone numbers should I keep handy in case of an emergency?

4 What is the Heimlich maneuver, and how do I do it?

5 What items should I keep in a first-aid kit?

6 What is the proper way to care for someone with a neck or back injury?

7 How can I protect myself or a loved one from allergic reactions?

8 What is the first thing I need to do when approaching an accident victim?

9 What is the best way to stop severe bleeding?

10 How do I check someone's pulse?

chapter
five

HOW DO I
TREAT BURNS?

Burns are categorized in three degrees: first, second, and third. First-degree burns damage the outermost layer of skin. The skin will look red and swollen, and it will feel tender. First-degree burns are usually considered minor. You may not have to call for professional medical assistance for this type of burn unless it covers a large portion of the body or affects the body's most delicate areas, such as the face or groin.

Second-degree burns damage the top two layers of skin and are usually quite painful. The skin becomes red and splotchy, and blisters develop. Second-degree burns that affect 1 percent of the body or less are considered minor and may not require medical attention. If more than 1 percent of the body is burned, they are categorized as major burns. Second-degree burns that affect more than 60 percent of the body can be fatal.

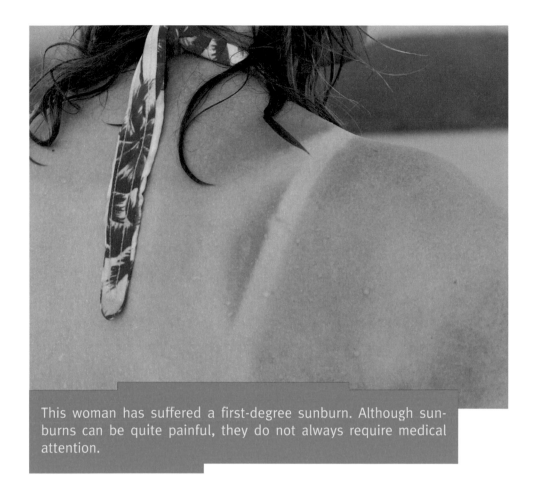

This woman has suffered a first-degree sunburn. Although sunburns can be quite painful, they do not always require medical attention.

Third-degree burns affect all layers of skin and may even reach the fat, muscle, and bone beneath the skin. Third-degree burns are painless at first because they kill nerve endings. The victim may not even know how badly he or she is injured. The burned area may look white, or it may be charred black. Third-degree burns caused by large fires may be accompanied by other complications, including smoke inhalation. Third-degree burns require immediate emergency medical attention.

Major Burns

Immediately call 911 in the event of a major burn. While waiting for medical professionals to arrive, you can take the following steps to help the victim. Make sure that the person is no longer in contact with the source of the burn, and check his or her breathing and heart rate. Make the victim as comfortable as possible. Elevate the burned area above the heart, if possible. Do not remove burned clothing, which may be stuck to the injured area. If you try to peel it off, the clothing may take skin with it. Drape cool, moist, sterile bandages or towels over the burned area, and keep the dressings damp until help arrives.

Type of Burn	What It Is Caused By
Dry burn	Flames, hot objects, friction
Scald	Hot liquids, steam
Electrical	Electricity, lightning
Chemical	Acids, bases, solvents
Radiation	Sun, tanning beds

Treating Burns

Before coming to the aid of someone who has been burned, inspect the surrounding area to make sure that you are not in danger of being burned or injured as well. Never rush into a burning building to help someone who is injured. Let firefighters attempt all rescues, and stay out of their way while they do

Children watch from a safe distance as firefighters respond to a house fire in Santa Ana, California. Firefighters wear fire-resistant clothing and breathing masks to protect themselves when responding to a fire.

so. Not only is there a risk of being burned yourself, but you can also inhale hot and suffocating smoke or toxic fumes. In the case of electrical burns, always inspect the area for live electrical wires. Don't touch the victim if he or she is still in contact with an electrical source. Wait for a professional to tell you that the electrical source has been shut off. You may need to move the person away from an electrical source or move the source itself (i.e., a live wire). However, this is highly danger- ous and should only be attempted when someone's life is in immediate danger.

The same goes for chemical burns. Before approaching a victim, make absolutely sure that you will not come into contact with the substance that caused the burns. Be cautious of toxic fumes that, depending on the chemical or gas, cannot always be seen or even smelled in the air. As always, call 911 as soon as possible.

When treating burns, don't ever use ointments or butter, which will only trap heat under the skin and increase the damage. Don't use ice to treat burns; this can result in frostbite. Don't break blisters. Broken skin is more painful and can become infected. A scald is a burn caused by very hot water or steam. Treatment for scalds is similar to that used for dry burns. Scalds usually result in more blisters than dry burns, so care must be taken not to break them.

Electrical Burns

On the surface, electrical burns may not seem that bad, but they can cause deep internal damage. A strong electrical shock can cause the victim to fall down or even be thrown away from the source of the shock. This may result in other injuries, such as cuts and broken bones. Electrical burns may also result in third-degree burns, unconsciousness, respiratory failure, and cardiac arrest. So it's important to check the victim's breathing and heart rate as soon as it's safe to do so. Other symptoms may include numbness, shock, and seizures.

Before treating someone with electrical burns, call 911 and make sure that the person is no longer in contact with the electrical source. When the person is safe to approach, lay the

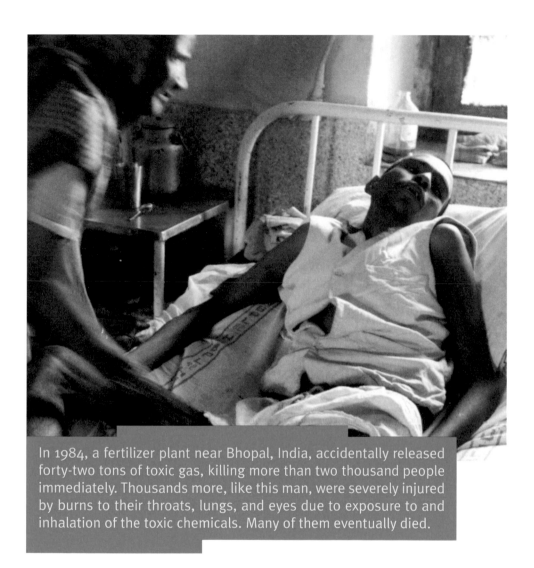

In 1984, a fertilizer plant near Bhopal, India, accidentally released forty-two tons of toxic gas, killing more than two thousand people immediately. Thousands more, like this man, were severely injured by burns to their throats, lungs, and eyes due to exposure to and inhalation of the toxic chemicals. Many of them eventually died.

person so that his or her feet are elevated to improve blood flow to the brain and help prevent shock. Gently cover the affected area with a dry, sterile bandage. Don't use blankets or towels, which can cause irritation. Monitor the person's breathing and heart rate until help arrives.

Chemical Burns

Chemical burns occur when caustic (harsh and corrosive) chemicals come into contact with exposed tissues. Substances that can cause chemical burns include acids, alkalis, cleansers, and solvents. Depending on the substance, chemical burns may cause immediate pain or they may go unnoticed for a short period of time. The burns caused by chemicals may look swollen and red, and blisters may develop. Sometimes the skin may become discolored. Chemical burns may be accompanied by intense, stinging pain. Internal burns may occur when chemicals are inhaled or ingested. Try to find out what type of chemical caused the burn so that medical professionals know how to treat the victim. Wear gloves when treating a person who has a chemical burn.

Chemical burns can get worse the longer the chemical is in contact with tissues. It's vital to flush the affected area with cool water for up to twenty minutes while waiting for help to arrive. If the chemical is a powder, brush residues from the skin before flushing. Carefully remove contaminated clothing and jewelry.

CHAPTER SIX

HOW DO I TREAT HEAT AND COLD EMERGENCIES?

The human body functions best at 98.6 degrees Fahrenheit (37 degrees Celsius). This temperature is called core temperature or human body temperature. Several biological processes regulated by the brain maintain it. Temperatures above and below core temperature can be harmful to a person's health or even fatal. In all emergencies caused by extreme temperatures, it's vital to remove or protect the victim from the source of heat or cold and restore normal body temperature.

Dehydration

During hot and humid days, people who work outside or participate in sports must be careful not to overexert themselves. They might become dehydrated, which is

On a day with temperatures in the nineties, this construction worker fights heat and dehydration by pouring a hatful of cool water over his head before going back to work.

when the body loses more fluids than it takes in. The body sweats to help keep its core temperature down. However, our bodies lose water when we sweat. We also lose electrolytes, which help regulate the fluids in the body and are necessary for the proper functioning of nerves and muscles. When we lose more water and electrolytes than we ingest, we become dehydrated. Dehydration can lead to heat cramps, heat exhaustion, and heatstroke. These last two can be life threatening if they are untreated or if the victim is in poor health.

To avoid dehydration, drink water frequently. If you feel tired, out of breath, or dizzy, stop working and rest in a shady place. If someone you know becomes dehydrated, have him or her sit in a cool place and drink water or an electrolyte-rich sports drink. Do not drink caffeinated or alcoholic drinks, which can cause you to lose even more fluids.

Heat Cramps and Heat Exhaustion

Dehydration often contributes to heat cramps. To treat heat cramps, relax in a cool or shady place. Drink water or a sports drink. Slowly stretch and massage the sore muscles until the cramps go away. If they persist for more than an hour, contact a doctor.

Heat cramps are often an early sign of heat exhaustion, which is caused by a loss of water and electrolytes. It usually affects people who are not accustomed to working or exercising in hot, humid weather. People who are sick or have sunburn may also be at risk of heat exhaustion. Symptoms include headache, dizziness, nausea, sweating, pale skin, cramps, weak pulse, and difficulty breathing. If heat exhaustion is not treated, it can lead to organ failure and death.

When treating someone experiencing heat exhaustion, you need to cool the person down and rehydrate him or her. Do what you can to stop the victim from sweating, which will waste water and increase the effects of dehydration. Move the person to a cool place and call 911 immediately. Have the person lie down with his or her feet elevated to improve blood flow to the brain. Remove tight or heavy clothing to allow heat to escape the person's body. Give him or her water or sports drinks. Carefully monitor the person to make sure that his or her breathing and heart rate remain stable.

Heatstroke

When the body produces or absorbs more heat than it can release, heatstroke may occur. Heatstroke happens when a person's body temperature reaches 104°F (40°C) or higher. This condition is different from a fever, which is the body's way of fighting infection and other illnesses. Heatstroke can follow heat exhaustion, or it can happen quickly and with little warning. Symptoms include heavy sweating, flushed skin, muscle cramps, difficulty breathing, faintness, headache, rapid pulse, and nausea. More severe symptoms include seizures, unconsciousness, coma, and death.

The first step in treating heatstroke is to call 911 immediately. Next, it's crucial to lower the victim's body heat as soon as possible. In addition to sitting in a cool place and sipping cool water, you may need to wrap the victim in a wet sheet and keep it wet until his or her body temperature drops below 100.4°F (38°C). When this happens, replace the wet sheet with a dry one, but be prepared to go back to the wet sheet if the victim's temperature rises again. If you don't have a wet sheet, fan the victim constantly and/or swab his or her head, chest, arms, and legs with a cool, damp sponge. Carefully monitor the person's heart rate and breathing.

Frostbite

Have you ever played outside on a cold winter day? After a while, your gloves and boots probably got a little wet, and your fingers and toes may have started to tingle or feel numb. The tingling sensation you experience in this situation is the very beginning of frostbite, or a freezing of tissues exposed to very cold temperatures. It usually begins in the extremities (body parts farthest from the heart): fingers, toes, ears, nose, and cheeks. Frostbite can spread up the arms and legs if it's untreated. Any part of the body that is exposed to freezing temperatures can develop frostbite.

When a part of your body is exposed to freezing weather, the brain sends signals to the blood vessels there, telling them to constrict, or grow narrower. This slows the flow of blood to the freezing tissues and sends it to more vital organs. Less blood passes through the exposed tissues, which keeps the blood warmer. The result is a drop in temperature in the

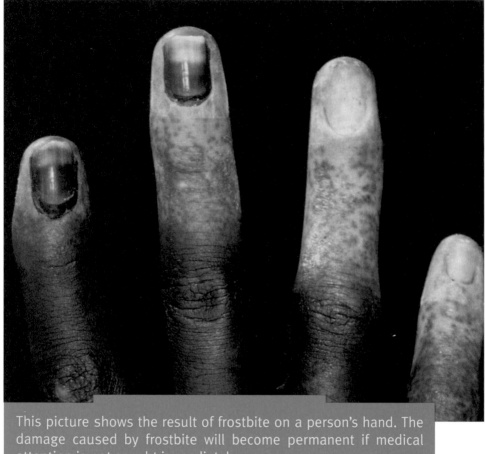

This picture shows the result of frostbite on a person's hand. The damage caused by frostbite will become permanent if medical attention is not sought immediately.

exposed body part. If the affected body part remains exposed, the blood vessels dilate, or widen, for a short period to let some blood and warmth reach the area. After this occurs several times, the vessels remain shut to protect the body against hypothermia (see next section).

Initially, frostbite makes the skin feel itchy, tingly, or numb. If frostbite is allowed to continue, the skin may feel like it's

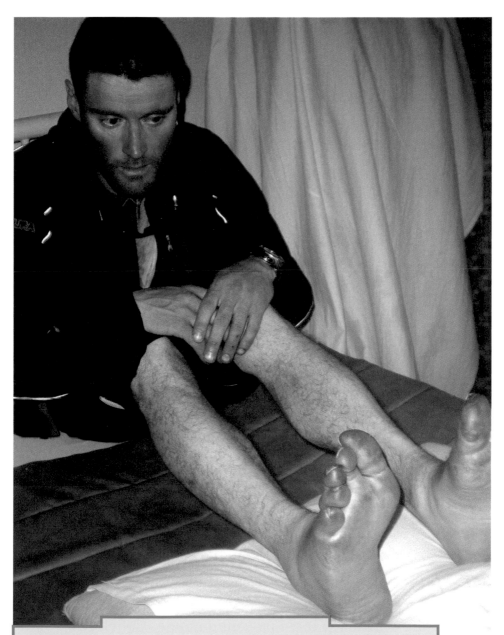

Marco Confortola, an Italian mountain climber, developed frostbite during an attempt to reach the summit of K2, the earth's second-tallest mountain. Eleven other climbers died during the same expedition due to an avalanche.

burning, especially when rubbed. In exposed skin, the space around cells freezes and can cause cell death. More cells are damaged or die because of a lack of oxygen caused by the reduced blood flow.

Freezing of blood vessels causes holes to form in them. When the area warms up again and the blood flow resumes, blood leaks out of these holes and forms blood clots. Warming a frostbitten area results in a throbbing sensation that can last for weeks as the body works to repair damaged tissues. After a while, the damaged tissues can turn purple and then black. Tissues that are starved of blood and oxygen for a period of time are also in danger of developing gangrene. This is tissue decay that can result in the removal of affected tissue, amputation of limbs, or even death if it's left unchecked.

Treating Frostbite

After contacting a medical professional, move the frostbite victim to a warm area and keep the affected area elevated to reduce swelling. Carefully remove constrictive jewelry and clothing. Gently wrap the affected area with sterile gauze, and place cotton between the fingers or toes to keep them from rubbing together. The victim can have warm, nonalcoholic beverages to help warm up his or her core.

Never rub frostbite. The friction can cause more damage. In fact, don't warm the affected area if there is a chance of refreezing, which will increase cell damage. Quick rewarming and maintenance of temperature is the best treatment for frostbite, so you need to get the person to a hospital or emergency room as soon as possible so that proper warming can occur. If you cannot get to a hospital, you may need to rewarm the affected area in warm water. Don't use hot water.

Hypothermia

Hypothermia occurs when more heat escapes the body than it can produce. It occurs when the internal body temperature drops below 95°F (35°C). People who enjoy outdoor activities in winter are at risk of developing hypothermia, especially when they are wet and cold for an extended period of time. Being immersed in cold water, even for a short while, can result in hypothermia as well. Very young and very old people are more likely to develop hypothermia.

The symptoms of hypothermia usually develop slowly and are sometimes overlooked until the problem becomes very serious and even life threatening. Initial symptoms include shivering and a lack of coordination. Other symptoms include cold skin, slowed breathing, slurred speech, and fatigue. Severe hypothermia can lead to cardiac arrest, respiratory failure, coma, and death.

Treating Hypothermia

If you suspect that someone has hypothermia, call for medical help immediately. Next, it's very important to move the person out of the cold. Replace wet clothing with warm, dry clothes or blankets. Cover the head to reduce heat loss. Do not apply direct heat. Provide a warm beverage, but never give the person alcohol. Monitor the person's breathing until help arrives.

Treat the person as gently as you can, and avoid moving him or her unnecessarily.

If you are stuck outside, do what you can to shield the victim from the cold and wind. Start a fire if possible, and remove the person's wet clothes. Wrap him or her in warm, dry blankets or clothing, and protect the victim from the cold ground by having him or her lie face up on a blanket. In an extreme situation, you may need to warm the person with your own body heat.

Myths and Facts

If someone is choking, slapping the back will help dislodge the blockage.

Fact: ➜ Slapping a choking person on the back may help, but it may also make things worse. It can make the blockage go deeper into the person's trachea, making it more difficult to expel.

Tweezers are the best way to remove the stinger after a bee sting.

Fact: ➜ Tweezers (or pinching the stinger with your fingers) might actually squeeze more venom out of the stinger, increasing the chance of a potentially deadly allergic reaction. Instead, use a credit card or your fingernail to quickly and cleanly scrape out the stinger.

Butter is a good treatment for burns.

Fact: ➜ Applying butter to burns traps heat under the skin and makes the damage worse.

Glossary

administer To give somebody something, such as medication or medical treatment.

adrenaline A hormone secreted by the adrenal glands in times of excitement or stress; also called epinephrine.

antibiotic A substance that can kill bacteria in the body.

artery A muscular blood vessel that carries blood from the heart to another part of the body.

binge drinking Consuming five or more alcoholic drinks in a short period of time (one to three hours).

cardiac arrest The abrupt cessation of blood flow due to heart failure.

disinfect To clean something to destroy disease-carrying microorganisms.

electrolytes Salts in the body that help regulate fluid levels and other body functions.

gangrene The localized death and decay of the tissues of the body that results from a lack of blood to the area.

immunization A medical treatment, usually given by injection, to make somebody resistant to a particular disease.

infection The reproduction of harmful microorganisms in the body.

ointment A smooth, greasy substance used to soothe sore, dry, or itchy skin and help heal wounds.

paralysis Loss of movement as a result of muscle or nerve damage.

rabies A severe viral disease that affects the central nervous system of most warm-blooded animals; it's transmitted by the saliva of infected animals.

resuscitation The process of reviving someone from unconsciousness.

seizure A sudden attack of illness that includes abnormal electrical discharges in the brain.

splint A strip of rigid material that is used to keep a broken bone from moving.

sterile Free from living bacteria and other harmful microorganisms.

tetanus A condition that affects the nervous system and causes painful, uncontrolled muscle spasms.

trachea The tube in oxygen-breathing animals that conducts air from the throat to the lungs.

American Association of Poison Control Centers (AAPCC)
3201 New Mexico Avenue, Suite 330
Washington, DC 20016
(800) 222-1222
Web site: http://www.aapcc.org
  The AAPCC is a private organization that manages the
  sixty-one U.S. poison control centers. It also manages the
  twenty-four-hour poison emergency hotline listed above.

American Heart Association
National Center
7272 Greenville Avenue
Dallas, TX 75231
(800) AHA-USA-1 (242-8721)
Web site: http://www.americanheart.org
  This voluntary health organization is dedicated to
  educating people about, and reducing the cases of, car-
  diovascular diseases and stroke in the United States.

American Medical Association (AMA)
515 North State Street
Chicago, IL 60610
(800) 621-8335
Web site: http://www.ama-assn.org

The AMA is the largest association of physicians and medical students in the United States. It's dedicated to promoting the art and science of medicine for the betterment of public health.

American Red Cross National Headquarters
2025 East Street NW
Washington, DC 20006
(703) 206 6000
Web site: http://www.redcross.org
The American Red Cross is a humanitarian organization that provides emergency assistance, disaster relief, and first-aid education inside the United States.

Canadian Red Cross National Office
170 Metcalfe Street, Suite 300
Ottawa, ON K2P 2P2
Canada
(613) 740-1900
Web site: http://www.redcross.ca
The Canadian Red Cross is a humanitarian organization that provides emergency assistance, disaster relief, and first-aid education inside Canada.

Centers for Disease Control and Prevention (CDC)
1600 Clifton Road
Atlanta, GA 30333
(404) 639-3311 or (800) CDC-INFO (232-4636)

Web site: http://www.cdc.gov

The CDC is an agency of the U.S. Department of Health and Human Services dedicated to disease prevention and control, occupational safety and health, and health education intended to improve the health of U.S. citizens.

Web Sites

Due to the changing nature of Internet links, Rosen Publishing has developed an online list of Web sites related to the subject of this book. This site is updated regularly. Please use this link to access this list:

http://www.rosenlinks.com/faq/emer

For Further Reading

American Red Cross, and Kathleen A. Handal. *The American Red Cross and First-Aid Handbook*. New York, NY: Little, Brown and Company, 1992.

Krohmer, Jon R., medical editor. *American College of Emergency Physicians First-Aid Manual*. New York, NY: DK Publishing, 2004.

Shojai, Amy D. *The First-Aid Companion for Dogs and Cats*. Emmaus, PA: Rodale Books, 2001.

Thygerson, Alton. *First Aid, CPR, and AED*. Sudbury, MA: Jones and Bartlett Publishers, 2006.

Walker, Allen R., medical editor. *First Aid for Babies & Children Fast*. New York, NY: DK Publishing, 2006.

Zydlo, Stanley M., and James A. Hill, medical editors. *American Medical Association Handbook of First Aid and Emergency Care*. New York, NY: Random House Reference, 2009.

Index

About the Author

Greg Roza has written and edited educational materials for children for the past nine years. He has a master's degree in English from the State University of New York at Fredonia. Roza has long had an interest in scientific topics and spends much of his spare time tinkering with machines around the house. He lives in Hamburg, New York, with his wife, Abigail, and his three children, Autumn, Lincoln, and Daisy.

Photo Credits

Cover © www.istockphoto.com/Andrew Simpson; p. 6 © www.istockphoto.com/Eric Foltz; p. 7 © Tim Wright/Corbis; p. 8 © www.istockphoto.com/Jeanell Norvell; p. 12 © Ned Therrien/Visuals Unlimited; p. 15 © www.istockphoto.com/Leah-Anne Thompson; p. 19 © Dan Callister/Getty Images; p. 22 © Susan van Ellen/Photo Edit; p. 24 © Jim Varney/Photo Researchers: p. 27 © www.istockphoto.com/Jon Schulte; p. 32 © www.istockphoto.com; p. 35 © Newscom; p. 39 © www.istockphoto.com/Joel Carillet; p. 41 © Tony Freeman/Photo Edit; p. 43 © Pablo Bartholomew/Liaison/Getty Images; p. 46 © Mark Wilson/Getty Images; p. 50 © SIU/Visuals Unlimited; p. 51 © Zakir Abbas/epa/Corbis.

Designer: Nicole Russo; Photo Researcher: Marty Levick